Bibliographic information published by the German National Library:

The German National Library lists this publication in the National Bibliography; detailed bibliographic data are available on the Internet at http://dnb.dnb.de .

Imprint:

Copyright © 2016 GRIN Verlag, Open Publishing GmbH
Print and binding: Books on Demand GmbH, Norderstedt Germany
ISBN: 9783668298071

This book at GRIN:

http://www.grin.com/en/e-book/339791/e-commerce-big-data-big-security-and-the-value-for-customers-and-companies

Luche Jackson

E-commerce. Big data, big security and the value for customers and companies

GRIN Publishing

GRIN - Your knowledge has value

Since its foundation in 1998, GRIN has specialized in publishing academic texts by students, college teachers and other academics as e-book and printed book. The website www.grin.com is an ideal platform for presenting term papers, final papers, scientific essays, dissertations and specialist books.

Visit us on the internet:

http://www.grin.com/

http://www.facebook.com/grincom

http://www.twitter.com/grin_com

Contents

E-commerce: Big data, Big Security and the Value for Both Customers and the Companies ... 3

Problem statement and study significance 3

How big data and security improves experiences 4

How big data and security finds customers and value 4

    Powering the prospect of business with big data and security 5

    Rationale to analyze the relationship between Big Data and security/ privacy policy 5

    The importance of Big Data and security/ privacy policy topic in contemporary environment
    6

Big Data 8

    Definition 8

    The empirical application of Big Data in business 9

    An overview of Big Data functions in a Company 9

Privacy and Security 10

    Definitions 10

The online purchasing 13

Pros and cons of online purchasing from both the clients and firms perspective 14

    Advantages 14

    Disadvantages 16

Comparison between purchasing behavioral model before after e-commerce 17

The Influence Mechanism of Big Data on Consumer Behavior 18

Managerial implications related to Big Data 19

    1. What happens in a world of radical transparency, with data widely available? 19

    2. If you could test all of your decisions, how would that change the way you compete?. 20

    3. How would your business change if you used Big Data for widespread, real-time
    customization? 21

4. How can Big Data augment or even replace management?... 21

5. Could you create a new business model based on data?... 22

Four Big Data strategies 26

1. Performance Management 26

2. Data Exploration.. 27

3. Social Analytics 28

4. Decision Science 29

Practical implementation of the ISO/IEC 27001 by companies 31

1. Integrating multiple big data strategies. 31

2. Assemble a Big Data capacity. 32

3. Be proactive and create a Big Data approach. 32

Conclusion 34

References.. 38

Privacy 49

Internet shopping 50

E-commerce: Big data, Big Security and the Value for Both Customers and the Companies

Problem statement and study significance

In the contemporary world, data is currently woven into all sectors and functionalities of the global economy and economies of scale. Therefore, the modern economic activities could not merely have succeeded which is a striking similarity to other indispensable factors of production such as capital and tangible assets (Kauffman, Srivastava, & Vayghan, 2012: Loebbecke, & Picot, 2015). The usage of big data, which is an extensive pool of data accumulated to provide or discern behavioral patterns and better decision-making, has become the center of rivalry and expansion in firms, production enhancement, and the creation of exceptional value for the global economy through waste reduction and quality improvement of goods and services offered (Narver, & Slater, 1990). This study tries to find insight on how the implementation of big data and security can improve firm's performance value towards customers. Until now, the stream of data deluging our world has been a trend that only thrilled few data geeks. Currently, the world of data is at the inflection point. A study by McKinsey Global Institute (MGI) asserted that the absolute volume of data stored, generated and gathered for insight has become economically pertinent to both customers and firms (Manyika, Chui, Brown, Bughin, Dobbs, Roxburgh, Byers, 2011).

The Big Data and Security can have the ability to transform lives. They are robust comparable to the forces of competitiveness and efficiency of preceding trends in Information Technology investment and advancement. The same prerequisites that facilitated the waves of Information Technology-enabled innovation to power productivity, i.e., technological innovations trailed by embracement of complimentary management novelty, are in place for big data, and big data sophisticated analytics abilities and technology suppliers are expected to have spread impact on efficiency similar to other technologies providers (Mithas, Lee, Earley, Murugesan, & Djavanshir, 2013, p. 18).

It has become imperative for firms to take big data and its potentiality to create value. This scenario has been set up as a result of competition and market forces (p. 20). For instance, businesses operating by the adoption of big data amass the potential to boost their operation margins by more than 60 percent (Orlikowski, 2007). The e-commerce and digital marketing firms have high chances of gaining considerable benefits from the evolution of big data and security. The availability of large-scale raw data being offered by massive audiences has become an added performance value to the firm's overall experience regarding service provision to the consumers (Martin, 2015). Big data plays a significant role in the establishment of new profitable opportunities and enhancement of accessible, center value chains in marketing and e-commerce programs. Both initiatives utilize big data in the ultimate expansion of firm's contributions and improvement of costumers' satisfaction (Nunan, & Di Domenico, 2013, p. 516).

How big data and security improves experiences

Big data and security tap into the heart of the customer experience in the process of developing quantifiable ways towards the identification of improvement on customer experiences. Schroeck et. al. (2012) asserts that every single firm that utilizes data on wide scale site uses big data and security to improve the user experience. Numerous techniques can be executed to ensure improved performance value of the firm and thereby user experience (Spiggle, 1994, p. 491). Dynamic pricing is one of the tactics of big data that can effortlessly secure sales when incorporated users experience combined with their expectations (p. 502). Eventually, the primary goal is to improve sales volume and promote user satisfaction, which can be offered by data influencing tactics such as dynamic pricing (p. 503). In collaboration with more effectual, targeted, and combined marketing experiences, the holistic idea of customer experience can be improved with the assistance of big data (Tankard, 2012, p. 6)

How big data and security finds customers and value

Many firms are finding ways on how to improve and customer purchase, make it as frequent as possible and eventual commitment to purchases more swiftly (Sharma, Mithas, & Kankanhalli, 2014, p. 433). Big data and security provide insights regarding some of the most complex rationales regarding whether a customers might or might not complete a particular sale (p. 440). According to Sharma, Mithas, & Kankanhalli, this move will reduce the incorporation of extensive and tedious surveys or analysis of collected data from in-depth focus faction (2014, p. 441). Online mega companies such as eBay serve millions of customers and big data, and security played an essential task in the advancement of new user products and privatized or individualistic recommendations. Therefore, this scenario suggests that surveys cannot singularly determine something that is based on personalization (Szongott, Henne, & von Voigt,

2012, p. 3). Firms require detailed information to enable them in the marketing of their products in an innovative and more discernible ways. Big data and security do only help in creation of solutions such as the above but also in their implementation (p. 6).

A similar strategy is applied in the disbursement and ordering processes. Most consumers prefer a desirable, digital, application-based experience in the course of purchasing food and beverages from the local restaurant and other outlets, but such experience has a downside in case the application defaults to match the standards of the physical experience (Vaidhyanathan & Bulock, 2014, p. 29). Big data and security offer the solution to the best practices for structuring a viable payments solution as well as in the identification of core markets (p. 64).

Powering the prospect of business with big data and security

Firms are set to realize huge profits and satisfaction by utilizing big data and safety policies. When customers trust the company regarding how it uses their data as well as the data is utilized in the process of adding value opportunities for consumers, realization of new fresh products and services, or in improvement of existing relationship and interaction, there are numerous opportunities that big data can provide in the quest of improving customer experience (Ann Keller, Koonin, & Shipp, 2012, p. 4). Firms of varied sizes entirely depend on big data to offer accountable and improved experiences customers deserve, and such practice will remain prevalent as long as various industries realize continued big data effectiveness (p. 7).

Rationale to analyze the relationship between Big Data and security/ privacy policy

The terminology big data refers to an immense load of digital information accumulated by governments and various companies regarding people and their surroundings. Based on this definition, it a research by Barton & Court (2012) indicates that 2.5 quintillion bytes of data are created daily (p. 77). Barton & Court further asserts that 90 percent of this data around the globe has been set up in the past two years (p. 78).

The diversity, rapidity, and quantity of big data intensify the security and privacy concerns including data sources and formats diversification, extensive cloud infrastructures, high capacity inter-cloud transfer, and torrent state of data acquisition (Bennett, Giles, Halevy, Han, Hearst, Leskovec, 2013. p. 2537). The analysis of the relationship between Big Data and security and privacy policy is paramount as the usage of comprehensive cloud infrastructure, with software platforms diversification, stretch across vast computer networks, amplifies the possibility of a malicious attack on the entire system (p. 2538). Conventional security mechanisms which were adapted for small scale static data security (disparate to streaming) are insufficient. For instance, generation of too many outliers is usually detected during analytics of anomaly detection (Beskow, Friedman, Hardy, Lin, & Weinfurt, 2010). The Same case applies where there is a clear method for retrofitting attribution in the open cloud infrastructures. Therefore, streaming of data requires fast response time regarding security and privacy issues (Beath, Becerra-Fernandez, Ross, & Short, 2012, p. 18). Some of the challenges faced related to big data and security, and privacy concerns include:

- Scalable and composable privacy
- Security preeminent practice for non-relational data stores
- Granular access control
- Secure data storage and transactions logs point input validation/filtering
- preserving data mining and analytics
- Cryptographically enforced access control and secure communication
- Real-time security/compliance monitoring
- Granular audits
- Secured computations in spread programming structure (p. 20)

The importance of Big Data and security/ privacy policy topic in contemporary environment

In the contemporary world, everyone is taking notice of the importance of the big data phenomenon including the federal governments. In 2015 Federal Trade Commission (FTC) instructed nine corporations that deal with data brokerage to provide information regarding the data they have collected from consumers (Wamba, Akter, Edwards, Chopin, & Gnanzou, 2015, p. 234). Such action indicates that regardless of the emerging usage and benefits of big data to businesses there are significant privacy implications that require being addressed (p. 235).

The FTC action is directed specifically to data brokers who perform data collection and analyze it to determine consumer behavior (p. 236). This information is then auctioned to various organizations and individuals' looking to improve their consumer marketing strategies and sales volumes (Waller, M. A., & Fawcett, 2013, p. 77). Conversely, it is vital to appreciate the fact that the emerge privacy concerns regarding the usage of big data are not limited to traditional

6

data brokerage (p. 84). The Economist Intelligence Unit (EIU) study indicates that the on lead-ers of big data users are nineteen industrial sectors such as Technology sector, financial sector, pharmaceutical and biotechnology sector, the manufacturing sector, consumer goods sector, healthcare sector, and professional services (The Economist, 2011). This scenario is a sign that big data revolution has started, and it is spreading across all areas of the economy. This, on the other hand, affects consumers and necessitating data security and adoption of stringent privacy policies (Strawn, 2012, p. 26).

Another importance of big data and security and confidentiality policy topic is the aspect of quality or rather the accuracy of the data and particulars of how that data is used by the or-ganizations that might affect individuals negatively on the decisions made (Tankard, 2012, p. 5). Therefore, in the light of features of the big data, it is important to determine the degree of accuracy obtained on individuals before making decisions (p. 8). Some information which is acquired illegally infringes the right of specific individuals while other information is inaccurate (Wagner, 2012, p. 54). For example, research by Waller and Fawcett (2013) indicates that the accuracy of information obtained through social media websites (p. 77). The question raised here is can this information from social media and various web-based sources be used in vet-ting and ranking job applications or the price increment in medical insurance? Information from such profiles is basic and unverified including marital status, the level of education, age, or employment status (p. 84). Also, a typical scenario is observable in free email services where the users, agrees to the terms and conditions, becomes vulnerable as they relinquish big data collectors to some degree of privacy for data aggregation (Schroeck, Shockley, Smart, Romero-Morales, & Tufano, 2012).

A study conducted by Shah, Horne, and Capellá (2012) confirms that one of the most contro-versial privacy perceptions for companies is the idea of acquiring approval for personal data collection and usage (p. 23). If it were possible to start all over again from the inception of big data ideology, this could be an ultimate ground-rule (p. 25). However, Smith, & Shao (2007) suggests that the idea of asking people their permission to accumulate their personal infor-mation might no longer be viable due to the prior personal data that have already been gath-ered and widely shared (p. 89). The identification of every organization that might have pre-viously collected personal data on individuals remains the hard truth as it is impossible (p. 110).

Rajpurohit (2013) suggests that removal and purging of data are one of the practices that can help individual restore their control of their personal data that had been collected by companies (p. 29). However, big data users cannot accept to offer such a feature as this would be an acid test to whether consumers would buy the fact that their data is being used for useful purposes only. Data regulators should consider data removal as one of the ways to protect consumers' privacy (p. 31). Big data usage continuity poses many privacy concerns and therefore it is recommendable as its uses evolve, the initial technical design and system architecture should encompass functional capability that allows such deletions to be performed when necessary (Pantelis, & Aija, 2013, p.40).

Similarly, the performance of personal data anonymization is another effective way of ensuring personal information is extra palatable to consumers (Williamson, 2000, p. 595). Anonymization refers to the removal or deletion of any fields or attributes that identify someone (White, 2012, p. 205). Although this method seems suitable, it has proved to be ineffective and unviable. According to White, 87 percent of Americans can be easily identified while using only three pieces of information including gender, birth date, and ZIP code (p. 208). This information is usually available in public records making it suitable for such cases. However, regardless of anonymization in place, there is still the risk of re-identification likelihood of these consumers particularly in U.S. (p. 209). Therefore, with these issues and tactile measures in mind, the common ground to ensure security and privacy in this burgeoning era of big data brokerage are collection of reliable and accurate data and final interpretation of that data (p. 214).

Big Data

Definition

Big data refers to the capacity that permits various organizations to dig out value from the vast pool of information or data. Just like any other ability to extract value from something, it requires investment in technologies, pre-eminence, and processes (Koch, 2013, p. 6). According to the research by Martin (2015), big data services and technologies market projects a booming growth from $3.2 billion in 2010 to $16.9 billion in 2015 (p. 27).

The empirical application of Big Data in business

The big data technology has become one of the critical approaches for business to outperform their rivals (Boyd & Crawford, 2012, p. 662). In many businesses, built up contenders and new participants alike will influence data-driven procedures to develop, contend, and catch esteem (Brown, Chul, & Manyika, 2011, p. 24). In social services, data miners are investigating the wellbeing outcomes of pharmaceuticals when they were broadly validated, and finding advantages and dangers that were not apparent amid inherently more controlled clinical trials. Additional pioneering adopters of Big Data are utilizing data from sensors inserted as a part of items from kids' toys to contemporary merchandise to decide how these items are indeed used as a part of this present reality (Chang, Kauffman, & Kwon, 2014, p. 68). Such information then illuminates the making of new administration offerings and the configuration of future items (p. 70).

Big Data will make new development open doors and entirely new classifications of organizations, for example, those that total and dissect industry data (Cherif & Grant, 2013, p. 18). Huge numbers of these will be organizations that rest amidst expansive data streams where data about items and administrations, purchasers and suppliers, shopper inclinations and goal can be caught and examined (p. 26). Groundbreaking pioneers crosswise over parts ought to start forcefully to assemble their associations' Big Data abilities (Constantiou & Kallinikos, 2015, p. 44).

Notwithstanding the sheer size of Big Data, the constant and high-recurrence nature of the data are likewise critical (Davenport, 2006, p. 98). For instance, "nowcasting," the capacity to gauge measurements, for example, customer certainty, quickly, something which already must be done reflectively, is turning out to be broadly utilized, adding impressive energy to prospect (p. 105). Moreover, the high recurrence of data permits clients to test speculations in close continuous and to a level at no other time conceivable (Davenport, 2010, p. 5).

An overview of Big Data functions in a Company

Big Data can open tremendous worth by making data straightforward (Davenport, 2012, p. 12). There is still a lot of data that is not yet captured in electronic structure, e.g., data on paper, or not made effortlessly open and searchable through systems (Davenport, & Harris, 2007). Bose (2009) ascertain that up to 25 percent of the exertion in some specialist information workgroups comprises of hunting down data and after that exchanging them to another (occasionally virtual) area (p. 155). This effort offers a unique wellspring of wastefulness (p. 172).

As associations make and store more value-based data in a computerized structure, they can gather more exact and point by execution point data on everything from item inventories to wiped out days and in this manner uncover variability and help implementation (Bialobrzeski, Ried, & Dabrock, 2012, p. 285). Indeed, some driving organizations are utilizing their capacity to gather and dissect big data to direct controlled analyses to settle on better administration choices (Biesdorf, Court, & Willmott, 2013). Big Data permits ever-smaller division of clients and in this way substantially more decisively customized items or policies (Demirkan & Delen, 2012). An advanced examination can generously enhance primary leadership, minimize hazards, and uncover valuable experiences that would somehow or another stay covered up (Ezzy, 2002). Big Data can be utilized to build up the up and coming era of items and administrations (Frost & Strauss, 2013). For example, makers are utilizing data got from sensors implanted in items to make inventive after-deals administration offerings, for example, proactive support to stay away from failures in new projects (Gefen, 2002, p. 30).

Privacy and Security

Definitions

Protection can be seen as a limit control process where an individual characterize with whom he will convey and what kind of correspondence (and the amount of) will happen (Chellappa & Sin, 2005, p. 668). Limit control empowers the particular individual to accomplish the coveted level of contact with others, at a given moment and as indicated by expressed conditions. Online protection is as needs be characterized as a trade of Internet clients' close to home data for a few advantages (Bigne, 2005).

The term online security is associated with data protection and in this manner is described as Internet clients' worries in regards to their capacity to control the gathering of their data, and in addition to managing the future utilization of the gathered data or the data that were produced in light of their online exercises (Kiron, Prentice, & Ferguson, 2014). Then again, data security can be characterized as an order that uses the ideas of privacy, trustworthiness, and accessibility to answer the subject of how data ought to be ensured.

Importance of privacy and security in today's business specifically on online purchasing

This CIA group of three is upheld utilizing different defensive instruments like encryption, validation, interruption recognition and so forth (Kalakota, & Whinston, 1997, p. 29). Questions that ought to be addressed when managing the insurance of data security are:

• Are the data shielded from being uncovered to people that ought not to get to them?

• Are the data shielded from being made, changed or erased by individuals that don't have authorization for these exercises?

• Are the data accessible to the individuals who need them?

If an organization cannot keep up the security of the data that it has gathered from its clients through online channels, then it is apparent that the organization is not meeting the requested level of corporate obligation (Koirala, 2012, p. 18). Online clients are progressively getting themselves presented to security dangers amid their online exercises. Security uncertainties incorporate the dangers like control with data and systems (e.g. demolition, offering or alteration of data) or different sorts of extortion and abuse (Lane, 2012, p. 40). Online security is characterized as online clients' view of how they are shielded from dangers identified with security. Reference utilized the term Perceived Security Protection (PSP) to depict purchasers' discernment that the Internet seller will satisfy security necessities, (for example, confirmation, uprightness, and encryption) (LaValle, Lesser, Shockley, Hopkins, & Kruschwitz, 2011, p. 22).

As the Internet is turning into an important portion of individuals' lives, more organizations utilize the Internet for business (Kung, Gordon, Lin, Shayo, & Dyck, 2013). This situation commenced with the transmission of a lot of data where the limit for putting away, recovering and checking data apparently rises. Clearly, the Internet has two unique appearances. One empowers energizing open doors for people to work systematically and spread their thoughts on the web. Alternate makes individuals powerless and keeps them from taking part similarly in an online environment (De Swert, 2012). Online clients " the exchange impacts conduct offs between what one surrenders (like divulgence or some likeness thereof of data) and what one addition from it (benefits like a day in and day out the accessibility of administration, efficient or different accommodations) (Johnson, 2012, p. 20). In the meantime, expanded danger in online situations is currently perceived in an extensive variety of threats that look to target online clients and endeavor data explicitly about them (Kim, Ferrin, & Rao, 2008, p. 545). A few studies propose that Internet clients have absolute protection and security concerns and that their trust has the essential part in the development of e-trade. Reference has examined the significance of four trust lists which impact internet clients purchasing intention and ability to give individual data. The included trust lists were: (1) alien protection seal, (2) protection explanation, (3) alien security seal, and (4) security highlights. The outcomes show that respondents' quality security includes the most (Griffin, & Danson, 2012, p. 98).

Shopping online is a standout amongst the most worthwhile things that present day innovation has managed us. For customers who do not care for the inconvenience of strolling around swarmed places or queuing in long lines, internet shopping is the best contrasting option to shopping centers and other open venues (George, Haas, & Pentland, 2014, p. 321). Also, lately, shopping online has turned out to be significantly more helpful through versatile installment arrangements. While you may appreciate scouring the Web for shabby methods in the solace of your home, you're shopping accounts and money related many prying eyes could bargain exchanges (Griffin, 2012, p. 44). Because of the system of e-trade and a large number of alternatives for online stores, sometimes it can be difficult to discern whether one is managing a real blue merchant or a counterfeit one.

Pretty much as customers need to take efforts to establish safety when shopping in block-and-mortar stores, online clients ought to likewise know about the dangers included with regards to online exchanges. In a perfect world, we as a whole consider securing our Mastercard data, and that is great (Yenisey, Ozok, & Salvendy, 2005, p. 259) However, that is not by any means the only security concern we ought to consider. In light of Data Privacy Day, there is a lot of emphasis on the significance of ensuring personal data protection with regards to shopping on the web. Web dangers are no more constrained to malware and tricks (Goes, 2014). Aggressors realize that the more people do any online exercises; they additionally expand the risk of uncovering more data about themselves, particularly when they are hoping to make a buy. Thus, hunting down things alone could lead people starting with one site then onto the next, and this expands the shot of discovering a pernicious one (Hayes, 2011).).

Since data breaks and episodes of hacking and widespread fraud are turning out to be more basic, online customers ought to ensure themselves against imminent attacks that could weaken their protection (Bubaš, Oreh ovački, & Konecki, 2008, p. 79). Various distinctive techniques can be utilized to attack a client's security, and eventually, an unsuspecting client will undoubtedly keep running into dangers, for example, phishing, online tricks, spam, Internet extortion, and noxious URLs (Mekovec, 2010, p. 195).

The online purchasing

Online purchasing refers to the acquisition of items and other services over the Internet (Black, 2005). English business person Michael Aldrich developed web shopping in 1979. Web shopping has drawn up in ubiquity throughout the years, mostly because individuals think that it is helpful and straightforward to deal shop from the solace of their home or office. A standout amongst the most alluring component about internet shopping, especially amid a Christmas season, is it lightens the need to hold up in long lines or scan from store to store for a particular thing. Web shopping (here and there known as e-tail from "electronic retail" or e-shopping) is a type of electronic trade which permits buyers to straightforwardly purchase merchandise or administrations from a dealer over the Internet utilizing a web program. Elective names are e-web-store, e-shop, e-store, Internet shop, web shop, web store, online store, online customer facing facade and virtual store. Portable trade (or m-business) portrays acquiring from an online retailer's versatile, streamlined online web page or application. An online shop brings out the physical relationship of purchasing items or administrations at blocks and mortar retailer or strip mall; the procedure is called business-to-customer (B2C) web shopping. For the situation where a business purchase from another company, the process is called business-to-business (B2B) web shopping. The biggest of these web retailing enterprises are Alibaba, Amazon.com, and eBay.

There are three stages of online purchasing include product selection, payment, and delivery. Product selection is made online where the customer chooses the products of choice. Payment is made using credit cards or online payment platforms such as Paypal, electronic payments, wire transfer, etc. Product and services purchased are delivered through shipping, drop shipping and in store pick up for physical items while downloading or digital distribution, printing and will call are used for digital items or services.

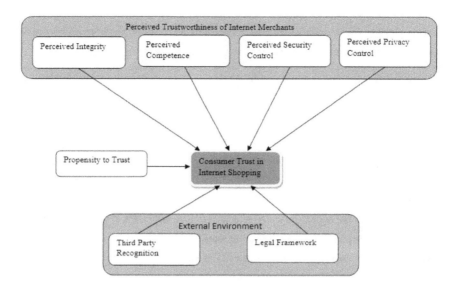

Figure 4: perceived trustworthy of internet purchasing

Pros and cons of online purchasing from both the clients and firms perspective

Below are advantages and disadvantages of online purchasing based on privacy policy management and security which is a fundamental topic to be analyzed from both clients' and firms' perspective

Advantages

Overcome geographical limitations: A physical store is confined by the geographical stretch that one can sustain. E-commerce makes the whole world a minimalized. Moreover, the advent of m-commerce, i.e., e-commerce on mobile devices, has dissolved every remaining confinement of geography.

Increase new customers with search engine visibility: Brand management and relationships drive physical retail. Notwithstanding these two drivers, online retail is additionally driven by activity from search engines. An extra source of movement can be the tipping point for some e-commerce businesses.

Lower costs: One of the most tangible positives of e-commerce is the lowered expense. A part of these reduced costs could be passed on to customers as discounted prices. Here are some of the ways that costs can be reduced with e-commerce:

Advertising and marketing: Organic search engine activity, pay-per-snap, and online networking movement are some of the advertising channels that can be practical.

Personnel: The robotization of checkout, charging, returns, inventory administration, and other operational means, lessens the number of operators needed to operate an e-commerce setup.

Real estate: This one is an easy decision. An e-commerce dealer does not require an extended physical area.

Locate the product quicker: It is no longer about pushing a shopping truck to the correct aisle, or scouting for the desired item. On an e-commerce website, customers can navigate intuitive route or use a search box to contract down their subject search immediately. Some sites remember customer preferences and shopping records to facilitate repeat purchase.

Eliminate travel time and cost: It is not uncommon for clients to travel long distances to reach their preferred physical store. E-commerce permits them to visit the same store for all intents and purposes, with a few mouse clicks.

Provide Comparison Shopping: E-commerce facilitates correlation shopping. Several online services permit customers to browse multiple e-commerce merchants and locate the best prices.

Enable coupons, deals, group buying, and bargains: Though there are physical equivalents to deals, deals, coupons, and gathering purchasing, online shopping makes it significantly more convenient. For instance, if a customer has a deep rebate coupon for turkey at one physical store and toilet paper at another, she may think that it's infeasible to the benefit from both rebates. However, the customer could do that online with a few mouse-clicks.

Provide abundant information: There are constraints to the measure of data that can be displayed in a physical store. It is hard to equip employees to respond to customers who require data crosswise over product offerings. Ecommerce websites can make extra data easily available to clients. The greater part of this data is provided by vendors and does not cost anything to create or keep up.

Creation of targeted communication: Using the data that a customer provides in the registration structure, and by embedding cookies on the client computer, an e-commerce merchant can access a considerable measure of data about their clients. This, thus, can be used to communicate relevant messages. An example: If you are searching for an individual item on Amazon.com, you will naturally be demonstrated postings of other comparative items. Furthermore, Amazon.com may likewise email you about related items.

Remain open all the time: Store timings are presently every minute of every day/365. Ecommerce websites can run consistently. From the merchant's perspective, this increases the number of orders they receive. From the customer's perspective, a "continuously open" store is more convenient.

Creation of markets for niche products: Buyers and sellers of niche items can think that it's hard to locate each other in the physical world. Rather than destroying older equipment for the absence of spares, today we can find parts online without lifting a finger.

Capacity to scale up rapidly: E-commerce businesses can scale up easier than physical retailers, as physical impediments do not bind them. Of course, logistics get tougher as one develops. However, with the choice of the right international logistics provider, one can scale up one's logistics as well.

Unlimited shelf space: Liberation from a physical store likewise entails being liberated from the confinements of shelf space. This permits e-commerce businesses to "stock" a broad range of items.

Disadvantages

E-commerce Lacks That Personal Touch: Not that every physical retailer have a personal methodology; however, several retailers appreciate the personal connection. As a consequence, purchasing at those retail outlets is reassuring and delightful. Tapping on "Purchase Now," and heaping up items in virtual shopping baskets, is simply not the same for me.

E-commerce Delays Goods: Unless you are utilizing a website to order a pizza online merely, e-commerce websites delivery takes a considerable longer time to get the merchandise into your hands. Even with express dispatching, the earliest you get products is "tomorrow." But if you need to purchase a pen because you need to write something at this moment, you can't purchase it off an e-commerce website.

Security: When making an online purchase, you have to provide in any event your credit card data and street number. Much of the time, e-commerce websites can harvest other data about your online behavior and preferences. This could lead to credit card extortion, or worse, identity theft.

Comparison between purchasing behavioral model before after e-commerce

The changes that B2C e-commerce has sparked ostensibly have had a more critical effect on the economy and on buyers' behavior than has B2B ecommerce. Previously, when consumers wanted to make purchases they needed to set aside time to shop amid certain hours of the day, or they needed to read through indexes sent to them via mail-order houses. Today, numerous consumers can just use their computers—and now advanced mobile phones or other portable electronic devices—to shop online. Buyers and sellers that engage in e-commerce retail trade are no longer restricted by store hours, geographic marketing areas, or list mailing records. With a few simple snaps they can access a variety of products 24 hours a day, seven days a week.

The characteristics of retail e-commerce merchandise additionally have changed fundamentally over the previous decade. In 2000, computer hardware was the most well-known type of merchandise sold over the Internet. Today, the variety of merchandise is extremely diverse, and shoppers can purchase just about anything online. Online shoppers have benefited in other ways. The development of e-commerce retail sales has reduced consumers' search cost, placed descending pressure on numerous consumer prices, and reduced price dispersion for some consumer merchandise. In any case, this has led to a generous decrease in the number of little companies operating in certain industries, as they tend to be less involved with e-commerce. Larger businesses, most outstandingly retail book outlets, new automobile dealerships, and travel agents, are better able to compete in this new market environment.

The extremely fast development of e-commerce retail sales has provided a noteworthy help to residential parcel delivery services. That is because online merchandise purchases involve some type of residential delivery by an outsider vendor, for example, FedEx, UPS, or the U.S. Postal Service. What's more, there appear to be considerable synergies related to B2C parcel and heavier freight volumes—parcel industry insiders have observed that businesses with solid e-commerce related B2C parcel shipment volumes often have stronger B2B shipment volumes than those that don't engage in B2C e-commerce.

The Influence Mechanism of Big Data on Consumer Behavior

Different from the conventional consumer behavior, in the era of big data, the amassing of large data and technology of C2C e-commerce model bring new influence. As stated earlier, the consumer's purchase decision mod-el has five stages. It is the same with shopping in customary shopping environment. The advent of the era of "big data", the use of massive gathering and technology is changing consumer behavior and feeling. Below is the examination of the characteristics and influence elements of consumers' online shopping behavior, and after that guide the online shopping behavior.

Rise of the Consumer as an Empowered Buyer: There have been numerous changes in consumer online shopping behavior, however one of the most critical abnormal state changes is that the internet has increasingly empowered shoppers over the most recent 20 years. Consumers began to realize they have more power because they had admittance to nearly an infinite number of merchants with nearly an infinite inventory over the globe, not simply nearby merchants in their home town. This meant they could take advantage of the wider selection and lower prices from merchants with better purchasing power or lower overhead. Consumers are no longer beholden to neighborhood merchants attempting to sell them their limited inventory at high prices. Indeed, Google's ZMOT study affirms that shoppers are in a great deal more control of the process than any time in recent memory. They are currently proactive consumers, needing to take more control purchasing what is offered to them, as well as looking for what they need, when they need it.

The Same Old Selling Model: Yet, every other e-commerce website still is based around merchants needing to sell you their stuff at their price. Amazon has a great selection, however the price is fixed - a couple of sunglasses is sold to you at the same price as me, even however I may have been willing to pay a great deal more than you because my need was greater. Even eBay sell-offs are another example of this because even in the event that I am the bartering winner, that was not the price I wanted to pay, that is the price forced upon me by the other bidders. What's more, eBay is selling the vast majority of their stuff at the Buy Now (fixed) price in any case, which is likewise not necessarily the price I need to pay.

The Big Data Flaw: One thing merchants have done very differently in the most recent 20 years is gathering data about consumers. I spent 11 years at Oracle, and have been an online marketer throughout the previous 25 years, so I am extremely acquainted with how demographics, psychographics, data warehousing, and examination are used in marketing. Be that as it may, I got frustrated because even with every one of these advances in technology over the last quarter century, and with the enormous measures of data gathered on consumer activities, most merchants are as yet improving just marginally guesses at what and when consumers will purchase and the price they will pay. Instead of attempting to guess, why not let the consumer tell you through their activities?

The Consumer-Driven Commerce Solution: I believe the answer for increasing revenue for merchants and true consumer fulfillment in this age of the empowered consumer is to permit consumers to take full control. Merchants ought to quit attempting to "sell"; quit attempting to guess what consumers will purchase and pay; and essentially permit consumers to purchase what they need, when they need it, and at the price they will pay. I believe this type of marketplace is the inevitable future of a more empowered consumer.

Managerial implications related to Big Data

The era of Big Data could yield new management principles. In the early days of professionalized corporate management, leaders discovered that minimum efficient scale was a key determinant of competitive success. Likewise, future competitive benefits are likely to accrue to companies that can not only capture more and better data but also use that data effectively at scale. We hope that by reflecting on such issues and the five questions that follow, executives will be better able to recognize how big data could upend assumptions behind their strategies, as well as the speed and scope of the change that's now under way.

1. What happens in a world of radical transparency, with data widely available?

As information becomes more readily accessible across sectors, it can threaten companies that have relied on proprietary data as a competitive asset. The real-estate industry, for example, trades on information asymmetries such as privileged access to transaction data and tightly held knowledge of the bid and ask behaviour of buyers. Acquiring both requires a significant expense and effort. In recent years, however, online specialists in real-estate data and analytics have started to bypass agents, permitting buyers and sellers to exchange perspectives on the value of properties and creating parallel sources for real-estate data.

Cost and pricing data are becoming more accessible across a spectrum of industries. Another swipe at proprietary information is the assembly by some companies of readily available satellite imagery that, when processed and analyzed, contains clues about competitors' physical facilities. These satellite sleuths glean insights into expansion plans or business constraints as revealed by facility capacity, shipping movements, and the like.

One big challenge is the fact that the mountains of data many companies are amassing often lurk in departmental "silos," such as R&D, engineering, manufacturing, or service operations—impeding timely exploitation. Information hoarding within business units also can be a problem: many financial institutions, for example, suffer from their own failure to share data among diverse lines of business, such as financial markets, money management, and lending. Often, this prevents these companies from forming a coherent view of individual customers or understanding links among financial markets.

Some manufacturers are attempting to pry open these departmental enclaves: they are integrating data from multiple systems, inviting collaboration among formerly walled-off functional units, and even seeking information from external suppliers and customers to co-create products. In advanced-manufacturing sectors such as automotive, for example, suppliers from around the world make thousands of components. More integrated data platforms now allow companies and their supply chain partners to collaborate during the design phase—a crucial determinant of final manufacturing costs.

2. If you could test all of your decisions, how would that change the way you compete?

Big Data ushers in the possibility of a fundamentally different type of decision making. Using controlled experiments, companies can test hypotheses and analyze results to guide investment decisions and operational changes. In effect, experimentation can help managers distinguish causation from mere correlation, thus reducing the variability of outcomes while improving financial and product performance.

Robust experimentation can take many forms. Leading online companies, for example, are continuous testers. In some cases, they allocate a set portion of their Web page views to conduct experiments that reveal the factors that drive higher user engagement or sales gains. Companies selling physical goods also use experiments to aid decisions, but Big Data can push this approach to a new level. McDonald's, for example, has equipped some stores with devices that gather operational data as they track customer interactions, traffic in stores, and ordering patterns. Researchers can model the impact of variations in menus, restaurant designs, and training, among other things, on productivity and sales.

Where such controlled experiments aren't feasible, companies can use "natural" experiments to identify the sources of variability in performance. One government organization, for instance, collected data on multiple groups of employees doing similar work at different sites. Simply making the data available spurred lagging workers to improve their performance.

3. How would your business change if you used Big Data for widespread, real-time customization?

Customer-facing companies have long used data to segment and target customers. Big Data permits a major step beyond what until recently was considered state of the art, by making real-time personalization possible. A next-generation retailer will be able to track the behavior of individual customers from Internet click streams, update their preferences, and model their likely behavior in real time. They will then be able to recognize when customers are nearing a purchase decision and nudge the transaction to completion by bundling preferred products, offered with reward program benefits. This real-time targeting, which would also leverage data from the retailer's rewards program, will increase purchases of higher-margin products by its most valuable customers.

Retailing is an obvious industry for data-driven customization because the volume and quality of data available from Internet purchases, social-network conversations, and, more recently, location-specific smart phone interactions have mushroomed. But other sectors, too, can benefit from new applications of data, along with the growing sophistication of analytical tools for dividing customers into more revealing microsegments.

4. How can Big Data augment or even replace management?

Big data expands the possible domains of application for algorithms and machine-mediated analysis. At some manufacturers, for example, algorithms analyze sensor data from production lines, creating self-regulating processes that cut waste, avoid costly (and sometimes dangerous) human interventions, and ultimately lift output. In advanced, "digital" oil fields, instruments constantly read data on wellhead conditions, pipelines, and mechanical systems. That information is analyzed by clusters of computers, which feed their results to real-time operations centers that adjust oil flows to optimize production and minimize downtimes. One major oil company has cut operating and staffing costs by 10 to 25 percent, while increasing production by 5 percent.

Products ranging from copiers to jet engines can now generate data streams that track their usage. Manufacturers can analyze the incoming data and, in some cases, automatically remedy software glitches or dispatch service representatives for repairs. Some enterprise computer hardware vendors are gathering and analyzing such data to schedule preemptive repairs before failures disrupt customers' operations. The data can also be used to implement product changes that prevent future problems or to provide customer-use inputs that inform next-generation offerings.

The bottom line is improved performance, better risk management, and the ability to unearth insights that would otherwise remain hidden. As the price of sensors, communications devices, and analytic software continues to fall, more and more companies will be joining this managerial revolution.

5. Could you create a new business model based on data?

Big Data is spawning new categories of companies that embrace information-driven business models. Many of these businesses play intermediary roles in value chains where they find themselves generating valuable "exhaust data" produced by business transactions. One transport company, for example, recognized that in the course of doing business, it was collecting vast amounts of information on global product shipments. Sensing opportunity, it created a unit that sells the data to supplement business and economic forecasts.

Another global company learned so much from analyzing its own data as part of a manufacturing turnaround that it decided to create a business to do similar work for other firms. Now the company aggregates shop-floor and supply-chain data for a number of manufacturing customers and sells software tools to improve their performance. This service business now outperforms the company's manufacturing business.

Five years ago, most companies collected data that were a part of their daily transactions and stored them in a database. This data was used primarily to keep track of operations or forecast needs. Today, both the sources and volume of data collected have exploded. It is now possible to collect click-stream data about every potential customer interaction with your web site. Marketers can also collect information about every conversation people are having about their brand. These sources of data have created modern-day treasure troves that can be mined to glean insights into products, services and customers. While this is conceptually possible, it requires the implementation of new processes, technology and governance mechanisms that are collectively being referred to as big data. Today, big data is big business.

Analysis which strategies and tools implement to increase online selling volume

In our work we have developed a framework (Figure 3) to understand big data strategies and the techniques used with each strategy. The main dimension that we consider is labeled business objective. When developing big data capabilities, companies attempt to measure or experiment. When measuring, associations know exactly what they are searching for and hope to see what the values of the measures are. When the objective is to experiment, companies treat questions as a hypothesis and use scientific methods to verify them.

The second dimension that we consider is labeled data type. In their ordinary course of working, companies collect data on their operations (e.g., sales) and capture it in their database that has a structure or schema. We call this value-based data. In other instances, companies deal with data that come from sources other than exchanges and are commonly unstructured (e.g., online networking data). This mix results in four quadrants, each representing a different strategy: performance management, data exploration, social examination, and decision science. We explain each strategy in the next section. (Figure 3 provides a rundown of prevalent big data techniques and vendors).

Figure 2: Big Data Framework

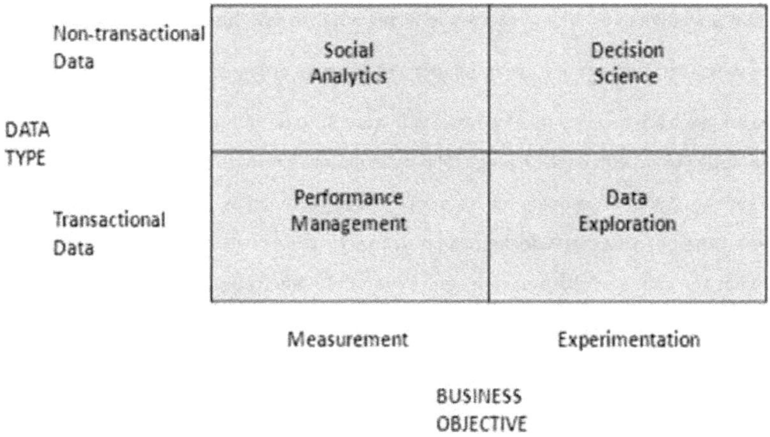

	Measurement	Experimentation
Non-transactional Data	Social Analytics	Decision Science
Transactional Data	Performance Management	Data Exploration

DATA TYPE (vertical axis)

BUSINESS OBJECTIVE (horizontal axis)

Figure 3: Popular Big Data Techniques and Vendors

	Technique	Vendor
Transactional Data	**Business Intelligence (BI)/Online Analytical Processing (OLAP):** • users interactively analyze multidimensional data • users can roll-up, drill-down, and slice data • BI tools provide dashboard and report capabilities **Cluster Analysis:** • segment objects (e.g., users) into groups based on similar properties or attributes **Data Mining:** • process to discover and extract new patterns in large data sets **Predictive Modeling:** • a model is created to best predict the probability of an outcome **SQL:** • a computer language that manages (e.g., query, insert, delete, extract) data from a relational database **A/B Testing:** • A method of testing in which a control group is compared to test groups to determine if there is an improvement based on the test condition • Often used in website design to test for higher conversion rates	**Leading BI Tools:** Microsoft SQL Server Analysis and Reporting Services SAP BusinessObjects Oracle Business Intelligence IBM Cognos/SPSS SAS Microstrategy QlikTech TIBCO Spotfire
Non-transactional Social Data	**Crowdsourcing:** • A process for collecting data from a large community or distributed group of people • Idea submission is a common crowdsourcing activity **Textual Analysis:** • Computer algorithms that analyze natural language • Topics can be extracted from text along with their linkages **Sentiment Analysis:** • A form of textual analysis that determines a positive, negative, or neutral reaction • Often used in marketing brand campaigns **Network analysis:** • A methodology to analyze the relationship among nodes (e.g., people) • On social media platforms, it can be used to create the social graph of follower and friends' connections among users	**Leading Social Listening Tools:** Radian6 Attensity Visible Technologies Converseon HootSuite NodeXL network graphs HP Autonomy Oracle Endeca IBM Watson

Four Big Data strategies

1. Performance Management

Performance management involves understanding the meaning of big data in organization databases utilizing pre-determined queries and multidimensional investigation. The data used for this investigation are value-based, for example, years of customer buying action, and inventory levels and turnover. Managers can make inquiries, for example, which are the most profitable customer segments and get answers in real-time that can be used to help make fleeting business decisions and longer term arranges.

Most business intelligence devices today provide a dashboard capacity. The user, often the manager or expert, can choose which queries to run, and can filter and rank the report yield by certain dimensions (e.g., region) and drill down/up on the data. Multiple types of reports and charts make it easy for managers to take a gander at trends. A big benefit for report developers is that they can interact with different aspects of business data including HR, marketing, sales, customer service, and assembling data, and get multiple perspectives of how the business is getting along.

BizTech, a leading data technology services firm in the Mid-Atlantic region, is planning to use business intelligence to help it develop sales. Founded in 2001 by Tom Connolly, BizTech's 2011 revenues were approximately $14M. Tom believes that critical improvement in measuring and reporting performance could help take BizTech to the next level of development. Specifically, BizTech arrangements to use Oracle's CRM-OD (On Demand) business intelligence application to improve its chance management process that involves generating, reviewing, and following up on leads. The organization's sales representatives and advisors will be able to generate new pipeline reports, including summaries by practice, regions, and sales representatives. These reports will be actively reviewed in weekly practice meetings, which will promote specific pipeline targets. What's more, learning from these reports can be tied directly to sales representatives' abilities development, honing, and recruitment strategy.

The uplifting news is the usefulness and ease-of-use of business intelligence instruments has improved greatly over the previous several years. On the off chance that designed and implemented effectively, these devices give managers a window into an immense measure of business exchanges that can help with their everyday decision-production. The principle challenge is to ensure that the quality and completeness of exchanges entered into the system or the result will be "garbage in, garbage out." Also, to guarantee a complete picture of the business, multiple databases crosswise over capacities have to be integrated.

2. Data Exploration

Data exploration makes heavy use of measurements to experiment and get answers to questions that managers won't not have considered previously. This methodology leverages predictive modeling techniques to predict user behavior based on their previous business exchanges and preferences. Cluster investigation can be used to segment customers into gatherings based on comparative attributes that might not have been on examiners' radar screens. Once these gatherings are discovered, managers can perform targeted activities, for example, modifying marketing messages, overhauling service, and cross/up-selling to each unique gathering. Another well known use case is to predict what gathering of users may "drop out." Armed with this data, managers can proactively devise strategies to retain this user segment and lower the beat rate.

With an increased emphasis on advanced, inbound marketing, associations need to pull in prospects to their website with engaging, strong, and targeted content. Running experiments, associations can test two webs sites, each containing different content, for example, white papers and demos, events, for example, webinars, and points of arrival and lead structure designs. The results of these experiments can help predict which blend of these variables twill lead to the highest conversion rate of site guests to qualified leads, and qualified leads to customers.

The large retailer Target used data mining techniques to predict the purchasing propensities for clusters of customers that were experiencing a noteworthy life event.2 Predicting customers who are experiencing big life changes, for example, pregnancy, marriage, and divorce, is vital to retailers since these customers are well on the way to be flexible and change their purchasing propensities, making them ideal targets for advertisers. Target could identify around 25 items, for example, unscented moisturizer and vitamin supplements, that when analyzed together, helped determine a "pregnancy prediction" score. Target then sent advancements focused on child related items to women based on their pregnancy prediction score. The result: sales of Target's Mom and Baby items pointedly increased not long after the dispatch their new advertising effort.

The rise in hearty measurable/explanatory techniques can lead to quick, direct results for data exploring associations. The big challenge is the absence of qualified analysts with expertise in the latest business systematic techniques. Another challenge is around data security/arrangement issues. Associations need to thoroughly consider the best approach to use the results of their data mining techniques to improve the customer experience, and not make customers feel that retailers are "spying" on them. For example, Target needed to conform how it communicated this advancement to women who were in all likelihood pregnant, once it had learned that the underlying advertising had made some of them upset.[2] As a result, Target made sure to include advertisements that were not child related so the infant promotions would look irregular.

3. Social Analytics

Social examination measure the unfathomable measure of non-value-based data that exists today. Quite a bit of this data exist on online networking stages, for example, conversations and reviews on Facebook, Twitter, and Yelp. Social examination measure three general categories: awareness, engagement, and verbal exchange or reach.[3] Awareness takes a gander at the exposure or mentions of social content and often involves metrics, for example, the number of video views and the number of followers or group members. Engagement measures the level of movement and interaction among stage members, for example, the frequency of user-generated content. More recently, mobile applications and stages, for example, Foursquare provide associations with area based data that can measure brand awareness and engagement, including the number and frequency of check-ins, with active users rewarded with badges. At long last, reach measures the extent to which content is disseminated to other users crosswise over social stages. Reach can be measured with variables, for example, the number of retweets on Twitter and shared likes on Facebook.

Social metrics are basic since they help illuminate managers of the success of their external and internal social advanced battles and activities. For example, marketing effort including contests and advancements on Facebook can be assessed through the number of consumer ideas submitted and the group comments related to those ideas. In the event that the metrics indicate poor results, managers can rotate and make changes. For example, low Facebook engagement may mean more interesting and interactive content needs to be created.

With recent advancements in social measurement techniques, we can now calculate one's "computerized impression" in the online networking world. Companies like PeerIndex and Klout can measure an advanced user's social influence. A Klout score ranges from 1 to 100, based on their calculation including number of followers, re-tweets, the influence of the followers themselves, and other variables. Marketers are utilizing social metrics to identify "influencers," those well-followed people who are talking about their specific image and can serve as a brand advocate. Utilizing Klout's services, Virgin America identified 120 people with high Klout scores and offered them a free flight to promote their new Toronto route.4 These people were not obligated to write about their experience. Be that as it may, between these 120 people and another 144 engaged influencers, the battle resulted in a sum of 4,600 tweets, 7.4M impressions, and coverage in top news outlets. Along these lines, the crusade created a high brand awareness of the new airline route.

Social analyzers need a clear understanding of what they are measuring. For example, a viral video that has been viewed 10M times is a decent pointer of high awareness, however it is not necessarily a decent measure of engagement and interaction. Furthermore, social metrics comprise of intermediate, non-budgetary measures. To determine a business sway, examiners often need to collect web activity and business metrics, notwithstanding social metrics, and afterward search for correlations. On account of viral videos, experts need to determine if, after viewing the YouTube videos, there is activity to the organization web site followed by eventual item purchases.

4. Decision Science

Decision science involves experiments and examination of non-value-based data, for example, consumer-generated item ideas and item reviews, to improve the decision-production process. Unlike social analyzers who concentrate on social examination to measure known objectives, decision scientists explore social big data as an approach to lead "field research" and to test hypotheses. Crowdsourcing, including idea generation and surveying, enables companies to pose questions to the group about its items and brands. Decision scientists, in conjunction with group feedback, determine the value, legitimacy, feasibility and attack of these ideas and eventually report on if/how they plan to put these ideas in real life. For example, the My Starbucks Idea program enables consumers to share, vote, and submit ideas regarding Starbuck's items, customer experience, and group involvement. Over 100,000 ideas have been collected to date. Starbucks has an "Ideas in real life" section to examine where ideas sit in the review process.

A large portion of the techniques used by decision scientists involve listening instruments that perform text and sentiment investigation. By leveraging these apparatuses, companies can measure specific points of interest around its items, and in addition who is saying what in regards to these themes. For example, before a new item is launched, marketers can measure how consumers feel about price, the effect that demographics may have on sentiment, and how price sentiment changes over time. Managers can then conform prices based on these tests.

In 2009, Whirlpool, the largest manufacturer of home appliances, wanted to discover what their customers and consumers were saying in regards to their items and services on online networking platforms.5 They used Attensity360 for constant observing and examination of conversations crosswise over prevalent channels, for example, Facebook, Twitter, and Youtube, review and blogger sites, and mainstream news. Attensity's text investigation discoveries were incorporated into Whirlpool's decision models to accurately predict customer beat, reliability, and fulfillment. This process enabled the organization to listen, respond, and measure on a scale unobtainable by manual methods. The results revealed that Whirlpool improved its understanding of its overall business. There was increased fulfillment, faster responsiveness, and overall, more satisfied experiences with customers. The organization likewise incorporated customer feedback to improve its item development and arranging process.

While technology has helped companies scale the listening process including social Big Data, the precision of listening apparatuses is nowhere near perfect. Manual work is needed to "prepare" these technologies on organization and industry-specific keywords with regard to textual and sentiment examination. Another great practice is to at first do parallel manual and listening device investigation to understand the exactness of the device and determine approaches to improve its effectiveness.

Practical implementation of the ISO/IEC 27001 by companies

Specific international standard about privacy management Standard ISO/IEC 27001:2005 helps organizations that deal with large volume of information secure that information. Standard ISO/IEC 27001:2005 contains the following aspects of information privacy management:

Information security policies

Organization of information security

Human resources security

Access control

Cryptography

Physical and environmental security

Communication security

Compliance

Supplier relationship

Information security incident management

Information security aspects of business continuity management

Asset management

Operations security

Systems acquisition, development and maintenance

1. Integrating multiple big data strategies.

While an organization can be effective with a single Big Data strategy, the best companies leveraging big data today are joining strategies. For example, one monetary establishment is leveraging both Social Analytics (non-value-based, social data) and Performance Management (business intelligence utilizing value-based data) strategies to guide its customer service. The bank generally determined its "top" customers based on metrics, for example, number and balance of records; these were the customers who received premium service. Presently, the bank is wanting to incorporate social metrics into the equation. Those online customers who are very active with respect to mentioning, engaging with, and advancing the bank on social channels will likewise be considered for abnormal state service programs. The money related foundation believes this is an a great deal more balanced approach to segment its most influential customers for customer service.

2. Assemble a Big Data capacity.

We define a Big Data capacity as the roles, technologies, processes, and culture needed to bolster big data initiatives. Perhaps the most reproachful of these are the roles, and specifically, the expertise and experience needed to devise and implement big data strategies. As mentioned earlier, multiple roles are needed: analysts who are skilled in the latest factual techniques; investigators and decision scientists who understand business measurement and experimentation and who can be the broker between analysts and business managers; the IT bunch who provides guidance on selecting big data technologies/techniques and who integrates business intelligence devices with value-based systems, for example, CRM and Web logical apparatuses; and business managers and knowledge workers who possess the business process and have to be comfortable with the new "language" of Big Data and social examination. What's more, some leading companies have created specific gathering structures focused on big data examination, and social content strategy and integration.

3. Be proactive and create a Big Data approach.

Companies need to keep up with policies and guidelines encompassing the use of Big Data, especially with non-value-based, social data that is often created and accessed outside organization dividers. Leading companies often have online networking policies and certificate programs/preparing regarding social data use. Big Data policies ought to likewise address issues regarding compliance, protection, and security. Leading associations clearly communicate and are honest in telling customers and consumers how they are utilizing personal data, for example, demographic data and past purchases. A rule of thumb that associations ought to take after is to dependably consider the customer/consumer/employee experience and their personal benefits from big data projects. Big Data projects that create a negative experience with users, despite the organization benefits, ought to be redesigned.

With the expense of data capture and obtaining decreasing at a fast rate, the real value of Big Data will be in its use. Companies that effectively create and implement Big Data strategies – , for example, those described above — stand to pick up a competitive advantage. Big data strategies need to take into record both value-based and non-value-based data. What's more, the concentrate needs to extend beyond utilizing Big Data to answer known questions, to experiment and discover trends that could help managers consider decisions and opportunities they would never have imagined before.

A good example of companies that have implemented ISO/IEC 27001 regarding specific international standard about privacy management is Amazon. To deliver valuable services Amazon utilizes propelled apparatuses to always alter valuing. This retailer can think about valuing data from contenders and consequently alter the cost of its own items. A few costs changes more than ten times each day. With the right web stages and modules it's simple. Dynamic estimating implies that organizations can no more contend by just offering the most reduced cost. There is currently like never before a genuine need to offer something more than worth, which implies retailers need to build up a decent notoriety and turn into the go-to alternative when a customers' needs a low cost and a decent affair. Personalized interactions are delivered more comprehensively as a result of improved clients trust in online purchases. Amazon is outstanding for utilizing big data to make item suggestions to customers. In the event that you have ever shopped on Amazon, you have most likely seen the 'Clients who purchased this thing additionally purchased' segment. Adding this straightforward element to item pages really brought about a 30% deals increment when the component was initially executed. This is a basic approach to help customers discover more items and to motivate individuals to invest more energy in a shopping site. People offering custom menswear online and are as of now taking a shot at making a database with data on men's body estimations and their style inclinations. They are likely to have the capacity to furnish a customer with items that fit their estimation once they enter their stature and weight despite the fact that they cannot gauge the person. The motivation behind this component is to make sure the right garments less demanding for the client and help them locate the right tailor-made thing. Amazon has been providing customers with better experiences which is evident by their current improves sales volume. Web clients are not as a matter of course agreeable about retailers thinking about their private lives, yet in all actuality big data will enhance the experience customers can anticipate from retailers. Big data is for case being utilized by Amazon and different organizations to search for conceivable fakes and ensure the personality of customers. Charge card extortion can be forestalled continuously on account of data assembled from live exchanges, geo data and social encourages. The way that a retailer knows some close insights about your life can appear to be odd, however big data is truly advantageous for organizations and customers.

Retailers can no more concentrate on contending on costs alone since they have the devices important to making a more charming, customized and consistent experience for customers. The figure below indicates the improvement of Amazon's sales volume after implementation of specific international standard about privacy management Standard ISO/IEC 27001:2005 in 2005.

Figure 4: Amazon growth in merchandise from 2004 to 2014

Conclusion

Big data examination (BDA) has emerged as the new frontier of development and competition in the wide spectrum of the e-commerce landscape due to the challenges and opportunities created by the data revolution. Big data examination (BDA) increasingly provides value to e-commerce firms by utilizing the elements of people, processes, and technologies to change data into bits of knowledge for hearty decision making and answers for business problems. This is an all encompassing process which deals with data, sources, aptitudes, and systems in order to create a competitive advantage. Leading e-commerce firms, for example, Google, Amazon, eBay, ASOS, Netflix and Facebook have already embraced BDA and experienced enormous development. Through its systematic review and creation of scientific categorization of the key aspects of BDA, this study presents a useful beginning stage for the utilization of BDA in emerging e-commerce research. The study presents a methodology for encapsulating all the best practices that assemble and shape BDA capabilities. Likewise, the study reflects that once BDA and its scope are well defined; distinctive characteristics and types of big data are well understood; and challenges are properly addressed, the BDA application will maximize business value through encouraging the pervasive usage and speedy delivery of experiences crosswise over associations.

On the off chance that the U.S. healthcare system were to use big data creatively and effectively to drive efficiency and quality, the sector could create more than $300bn in value every year. 66% of that would be a 8 percent reduction in U.S. healthcare expenditure. In the developed economies of Europe, government overseers could create more than €100bn ($123bn) in operational efficiency improvements alone by utilizing Big Data – and that is excluding employing advanced logical instruments to reduce misrepresentation and errors and support the collection of duty revenues.

However, it's not simply companies and associations that stand to pick up from the value that Big Data can create. Consumers can likewise reap exceptionally noteworthy benefits. For instance, users of services enabled by personal-area data can capture $600bn in consumer excess.

Take brilliant steering utilizing real-time activity data, which is one of the most heavily-used uses of personal-area data. As the penetration of advanced mobile phones increases, and free route applications are included in these devices, the use of shrewd steering is likely to develop. By 2020, more than 70 percent of mobile phones are expected to have a GPS capacity, up from 20 percent in 2010. On the whole, we estimate that the potential worldwide value of shrewd directing as time and fuel reserve funds will be about $500 billion by 2020. This is equivalent to sparing drivers 20 billion hours out and about, or 10 to 15 hours every year for each traveler, and about $150 billion on fuel utilization.

Some of the most huge potential to generate value from Big Data will come from consolidating separate pools of data. The U.S. healthcare system, for instance, has four noteworthy pools of data – clinical; action (claims) and cost; pharmaceutical and medical items R&D; and data about patient behavior and sentiment – each of which is principally captured and managed by a different constituency. MGI estimates that if U.S. healthcare completely used all the available techniques that can be enabled by Big Data, for example, dissecting records of real-world medical treatments, their expenses and health outcomes to guide doctors on which treatments provide the best outcomes at the best cost, the yearly efficiency of the sector could develop by an extra 0.7 per cent. In any case, achieving this help in profitability will require the mix of data from different sources – often from associations that have no history of sharing data at scale. Sets of data, for example, patient records and clinical cases would have to be integrated.

Doing as such would create benefits for the different business players as well as for patients, who might have broader, clearer access to a wider variety of healthcare data, making them more informed. Patients would be able to compare not just the prices of medications, treatments, and doctors, additionally their relative effectiveness, enabling them to choose more effective, better-targeted medicines, potentially even customized to their personal genetic and molecular make-up. To get those wide benefits, healthcare consumers may have to accept a marginally different trade-off between their security and the benefits that wider pooling of data would bring.

Sensitivities around protection and data security are only one hurdle that companies and governments need to overcome if the economic benefits of big data are to be realized. One of the most pressing challenges is a noteworthy shortage of people with the aptitudes to analyze big data. By 2018, the United States alone could face a shortage of 140,000 to 190,000 people with deep diagnostic preparing (in measurements or machine learning) and another 1.5 million people with the managerial and quantitative aptitudes to be able to frame and interpret analyses effectively enough to base decisions on them.

There are additionally numerous technological issues that need to be resolved to make the a large portion of big data. Legacy systems and incompatible benchmarks and organizations often prevent the integration of data and the utilization of the more sophisticated investigation that create value. Ultimately, making use of large computerized datasets will require the assembly of a technology stack from storage and registering through logical and perception software applications.

Above all, access to data needs to broaden. Increasingly, companies should access data from outsiders, e.g., business partners or customers, and integrate them with their own. An essential competency for data-driven associations in the future will be the capacity to create compelling value recommendations for others, including consumers, suppliers and potentially even competitors, to share data. In the event that it looks unlikely that data sharing will happen despite the potential for societal benefits (a market failure), legislators may then have to step in.

For whatever length of time that companies and governments understand the power of Big Data to deliver higher efficiency, better value for consumers, and the next wave of development in the worldwide economy, there ought to be a solid enough incentive for them to act powerfully to overcome the barriers to its use. By doing as such they will unleash avenues to new competitiveness among companies, higher efficiency in the general population sector that will enable better services, even in constrained monetary times, and enable firms and even whole economies to be more productive.

The emergence of the big data is a new challenge to in-arrangement security. On the off chance that consumers don't understand the big data, they would have a new stress. The convenience and speedy data search let consumers rely more on big data. Recommended Network provides more choices for consumers. They are more likely to believe post-purchase evaluation and other consumers. Consumers have been tired of the advertising effort. They are more likely to experience marketing, interest the personal experience and participate in marketing.

References

1.   Agarwal, R., & Dhar, V. (2014). Editorial—big data, data science, and analytics: the opportunity and challenge for IS research. *Information Systems Research, 25,* 443–448.

2.   Agarwal, R., & Weill, P. (2012). The benefits of combining data with empathy. *MIT Sloan Management Review, 54,* 35.

3.   Allen, B., Bresnahan, J., Childers, L., Foster, I., Kandaswamy, G., Kettimuthu, R., Kordas, J., Link, M., Martin, S., Pickett, K., & Tuecke, S. (2012). Software as a service for data scientists. *Communications of the ACM, 55,* 81–88.

4.   Ann Keller, S., Koonin, S. E., & Shipp, S. (2012). Big data and city living - what can it do for us? *Significance, 9,* 4–7.

5.   Bankston, K.S., Soltani, A., (2014). Tiny constables and the cost of surveillance: Making cents out of United States V. Jones. Yale Law Journal Online 123.

6.   Barney, J. (1991). Firm resources and sustained competitive advantage. *Journal of Management, 17,* 99–120.

7.   Barrett, M., Davidson, E., Prabhu, J., & Vargo, S. L. (2015). Service innovation in the digital age. *MIS Quarterly, 39,* 135–154.

8.   Barton, D. (2012). Making advanced analytics work for you. *Harvard Business Review, 90*(78–83), 128.

9.   Barton, D., & Court, D. (2012). Making advanced analytics work for you. *Harvard Business Review, 90,* 78.

10.   Beath, C., Becerra-Fernandez, I., Ross, J., & Short, J. (2012). Finding value in the information explosion. *MIT Sloan Management Review, 53,* 18–20.

11.   Benedettini, O., Neely, A., 2012. Complexity in services: An interpretative framework, POMS 23rd annual conference.

12.   Bennett, P., Giles, L., Halevy, A., Han, J., Hearst, M., Leskovec, J., 2013. Channeling the deluge: research challenges for big data and information systems, Proceedings of the 22nd ACM international conference on Conference on information & knowledge management. ACM, pp. 2537–2538.

13.   Beskow, L. M., Friedman, J. Y., Hardy, N. C., Lin, L., & Weinfurt, K. P. (2010). Developing a simplified consent form for biobanking. *PloS One, 5,* e13302.

14.   Beulke, D., (2011). Big Data Impacts Data Management: The 5 Vs of big data. URL: http://davebeulke.com/big-data-impacts-data-management-the-five-vs-of-big-data

15. Bhattacherjee, A. (2001). Understanding information systems continuance: an expectation-confirmation model. *MIS Quarterly, 25,* 351–370.

16. Bialobrzeski, A., Ried, J., & Dabrock, P. (2012). Differentiating and evaluating common good and public good: making implicit assumptions explicit in the contexts of consent and duty to participate. *Public Health Genomics, 15,* 285–292.

17. Biesdorf, S., Court, D., & Willmott, P. (2013). *Big data: What's your plan?* McKinsey Quarterly.

18. Birnik, A., & Bowman, C. (2007). Marketing mix standardization in multinational corporations: a review of the evidence. *International Journal of Management Reviews, 9,* 303–324.

19. Boja, C., Pocovnicu, A., & Batagan, L. (2012). Distributed Parallel Architecture for "Big Data". *Informatica Economica, 16,* 116–127.

20. Bose, R. (2009). Advanced analytics: opportunities and challenges. *Industrial Management & Data Systems, 109,* 155–172.

21. Bouhaddou, O., Bennett, J., Cromwell, T., Nixon, G., Teal, J., Davis, M., Smith, R., Fischetti, L., Parker, D., & Gillen, Z. (2011). *The Department of Veterans Affairs, Department of Defense, and Kaiser Permanente Nationwide health information network exchange in San Diego: Patient selection, consent, and identity Matching, AMIA annual symposium proceedings* (p. 135). American Medical Informatics Association.

22. Boyd, D., & Crawford, K. (2012). Critical questions for big data: provocations for a cultural, technological, and scholarly phenomenon. *Information Communication and Society, 15,* 662–679.

23. Bragge, J., Sunikka, A., & Kallio, H. (2012). An exploratory study on customer responses to personalized banner messages in the online banking context. *JITTA: Journal of Information Technology Theory and Application, 13,* 5–18.

24. Braun, V., & Clarke, V. (2006). *Using thematic analysis in psychology qualitative research in psychology, 3, 77–101.* Bristol: University of the West of England.

25. Brown, B., Chul, M., Manyika, J., (2011). Are you ready for the era of 'big data'? *McKinsey Quarterly 4,* 24–35.

26. Bughin, J., Chui, M., & Manyika, J. (2010). Clouds, big data, and smart assets: ten tech-enabled business trends to watch. *The McKinsey Quarterly, 4,* 26–43.

27. Bughin, J., Livingston, J., & Marwaha, S. (2011). Seizing the potential of 'big data'. *The McKinsey Quarterly, 4*, 103–109.

28. Chandrasekaran, S., Levin, R., Patel, H., Roberts, R., (2013). Winning with IT in consumer packaged goods: Seven trends transforming the role of the CIO. McKinsey & Company, pp. 1–8.

29. Chang, R. M., Kauffman, R. J., & Kwon, Y. (2014). Understanding the paradigm shift to computational social science in the presence of big data. *Decision Support Systems, 63*, 67–80.

30. Cherif, E., & Grant, D. (2013). Analysis of E-business models in real estate. *Electronic Commerce Research, 14*, 1–26.

31. Constantiou, I.D., Kallinikos, J., (2015). New games, new rules: Big data and the changing context of strategy. *Journal of Information Technology, 30*(1), 44–57.

32. Davenport, T. H. (2006). Competing on Analytics. *Harvard Business Review, 84*, 98–107.

33. Davenport, T. H. (2010). The New World of "Business Analytics. *International Institute for Analytics*, 1–6.

34. Davenport, T.H., 2012. The Human Side of Big Data and High-Performance Analytics. International Institute for Analytics, pp. 1–13.

35. Davenport, T. H. (2013a). Analytics 3.0. *Harvard Business Review, 91*, 64–72.

36. Davenport, T. H. (2013b). Keep up with your quants. *Harvard Business Review, 91*, 120–123.

37. Davenport, T. H., & Harris, J. G. (2007a). *Competing on analytics: The new science of winning*. Boston: Harvard Business School Press.

38. Davenport, T.H., Harris, J.G., (2007b). The dark side of customer analytics. Harvard Business Review 85, 37 – +.

39. Davenport, T. H., & Patil, D. (2012). Data scientist: the sexiest job of the 21st century. *Harvard Business Review, 90*, 70–77.

40. Davenport, T. H., Barth, P., & Bean, R. (2012). How 'Big Data'is Different. *MIT Sloan Management Review, 54*, 43–46.

41. De Swert, K., (2012). Calculating inter-coder reliability in media content analysis using Krippendorff's alpha. Center for Politics and Communication.

42. Delone, W. H. (2003). The DeLone and McLean model of information systems success: a ten-year update. *Journal of Management Information Systems, 19*, 9–30.

43. DeLone, W. H., & McLean, E. R. (1992). Information systems success: the quest for the dependent variable. *Information Systems Research, 3*, 60–95.

44. Demirkan, H., Delen, D., (2012). Leveraging the capabilities of service-oriented decision support systems: Putting analytics and big data in cloud. Decision Support Systems.

45. Devaraj, S., Fan, M., & Kohli, R. (2002). Antecedents of B2C channel satisfaction and preference: validating e-commerce metrics. *Information Systems Research, 13*, 316–333.

46. Dijcks, J. P. (2012). *Oracle: Big data for the Enterprise.* Oracle: USA.

47. Dimon, R. (2013). *Understand: Turning insights into actions.* Enterprise Performance Management Done Right: An Operating System for Your Organization, pp.57–77.

48. Dinev, T., & Hart, P. (2006). An extended privacy calculus model for E-commerce transactions. *Information Systems Research, 17*, 61–80.

49. emarketer, (2013). Ecommerce Sales Topped $1 Trillion for First Time in 2012. Available at: www.emarketer.com/Article/Ecommerce-Sales-Topped-1-Trillion-First-Time-2012/1009649 (Accessed 10 April 2013).

50. Ezzy, D. (2002). *Qualitative analysis: Practice and innovation Allen & Unwin.* Crows Nest: Allen & Unwins.

51. Ferguson, R. B. (2012). Risky business: how data analytics and behavioral science can help. *MIT Sloan Management Review, 54*, 1–5.

52. Fisher, D., DeLine, R., Czerwinski, M., & Drucker, S. (2012). Interactions with big data analytics. *Interactions, 19*, 50.

53. Fosso Wamba, S., Anand, A., & Carter, L. (2013). A literature review of rfid-enabled healthcare applications and issues. *International Journal of Information Management, 33*, 875–891.

54. Fosso Wamba, S., Akter, S., Coltman, T. W. T., & Ngai, E. (2015a). Guest editorial: information technology-enabled supply chain management. *Production Planning and Control, 26*, 933–944.

55. Fosso Wamba, S., Akter, S., Edwards, A., Chopin, G., & Gnanzou, D. (2015b). How 'big data' can make big impact: findings from a systematic review and a longitudinal case study. *International Journal of Production Economics, 165*, 234–246.

56.   Frost, R., Strauss, J., (2013). E-marketing. Pearson Prentice Hall. Upper Saddle River, NJ.

57.   Gantz, J., & Reinsel, D. (2012). The digital universe in 2020: Big data, bigger digital shadows, and biggest growth in the far east (2012). URL: http://www.emc.com/collateral/analyst-reports/idc-the-digital-universein-2020. pdf.

58.   Gefen, D. (2000). E-commerce: the role of familiarity and trust. *Omega, 28*, 725–737.CrossRef

59.   Gefen, D. (2002). Customer loyalty in E-commerce. *Journal of the Association for Information Systems, 3*, 27–51.

60.   Gehrke, J. (2012). Quo vadis, data privacy? *Annals of the New York Academy of Sciences, 1260*, 45–54.

61.   Gentile, B., (2012). Top 5 myths about big data. Available at: http://mashable.com/2012/06/19/big-data-myths/#MwZnjjrOR8qV (Accessed 2nd of March, 2016).

62.   George, G., Haas, M. R., & Pentland, A. (2014). Big data and management. *Academy of Management Journal, 57*, 321–326.

63.   Gobble, M. M. (2013). Big data: the next big thing in innovation. *Research Technology Management, 56*, 64–66.

64.   Goes, P.B., (2014). Big Data and IS Research. MIS Quarterly 38, iii-viii.

65.   Goff, J., McInerney, P., Soni, G., (2012). Need for speed: Algorithmic marketing and customer data overload, McKinsey Quarterly.

66.   Griffin, R. (2012). Using Big Data to Combat Enterprise Fraud. *Financial Executive, 28*, 44–47.

67.   Griffin, J., & Danson, F. (2012). Analytics and the Cloud - the Future is here. *Financial Executive, 28*, 97–98.

68.   Havens, T. C., Bezdek, J. C., Leckie, C., Hall, L. O., & Palaniswami, M. (2012). Fuzzy C-means algorithms for very large data. *Fuzzy Systems, IEEE Transactions on, 20*, 1130–1146.

69.   Hayashi, A. M. (2014). Thriving in a big data world. *MIT Sloan Management Review, 55*, 35–39.

70.   Hayes, A.F., (2011). My macros and code for SPSS and SAS. Retrieved September 27, 2011.

71.   Hayes, A. F., & Krippendorff, K. (2007). Answering the call for a standard reliability measure for coding data. *Communication Methods and Measures, 1*, 77–89.

72.   Highfield, (2012). Talking of Many Things: Using Topical Networks to Study Discussions in Social Media. *Journal of Technology in Human Services, 30*(3–4), 204–218.

73.   Holbrook, M. B. (1999). *Consumer value: A framework for analysis and research*. London: Psychology Press.

74.   Hsinchun, C., Chiang, R. H. L., & Storey, V. C. (2012). Business intelligence and analytics: from big data to big impact. *MIS Quarterly, 36*, 1165–1188.

75.   Hull, G. (2015). Successful failure: what foucault can teach us about privacy self-management in a world of facebook and big data. *Ethics and Information Technology, 17*(2), 89–101.

76.   Huwe, T. K. (2012). Big data, big future. *Computers in Libraries, 32*, 20–22.

77.   IBM, (2012). What is big data? Available at: http://www-01.ibm.com/software/data/big-data/what-is-big-data.html (Accessed 2nd of March, 2016).

78.   Ioannidis, J. P. (2013). Informed consent, big data, and the oxymoron of research that is not research. *The American Journal of Bioethics, 13*, 40–42.

79.   Jacobs, A., (2009). The Pathologies of Big Data. Association For Computing Machinery. Communications of the ACM 52, 36.

80.   Jao, J., (2013). Why big data Is A must In ecommerce. Available at: http://www.bigdatalandscape.com/news/why-big-data-is-a-must-in-ecommerce (Accessed 2nd of March, 2016).

81.   Johnson, B. D. (2012a). The secret life of data. *The Futurist, 46*, 20–23.

82.   Johnson, J. E. (2012b). Big data + big analytics = big opportunity. *Financial Executive, 28*, 50–53.

83.   Kalakota, R., & Whinston, A. B. (1997). *Electronic commerce: A manager's guide*. Reading: Addison-Wesley Professional.

84.   Kang, K.-D., Son, S. H., & Stankovic, J. A. (2003). Differentiated real-time data services for E-commerce applications. *Electronic Commerce Research, 3*, 113–142.

85.   Kaplan, B. (2014). *Selling health data: De-Identification, privacy, and speech*. Forthcoming: Cambridge Quarterly of Healthcare Ethics, 24(3):256–71.

86.   Kauffman, R. J., Srivastava, J., & Vayghan, J. (2012). Business and data analytics: new innovations for the management of E-commerce. *Electronic Commerce Research and Applications, 11*, 85–88.

87.   Kim, G., Shin, B., & Kwon, O. (2012). Investigating the value of sociomaterialism in conceptualizing it capability of a firm. *Journal of Management Information Systems, 29*, 327–362.

88.   Kiron, D., Prentice, P. K., & Ferguson, R. B. (2012a). Innovating with analytics. *MIT Sloan Management Review, 54*, 47–52.

89.   Kiron, D., Shockley, R., Kruschwitz, N., Finch, G., & Haydock, M. (2012b). Analytics: the widening divide. *MIT Sloan Management Review, 53*, 1–22.

90.   Kiron, D., Prentice, P. K., & Ferguson, R. B. (2014a). The analytics mandate. *MIT Sloan Management Review, 55*, 1–25.

91.   Kiron, D., Prentice, P. K., & Ferguson, R. B. (2014b). Raising the bar with analytics. *MIT Sloan Management Review, 55*, 29–33.

92.   Koch, C. (2013). *Compilation and synthesis in big data analytics, big data* (pp. 6–6). Berlin: Springer.

93.   Kohli, A. K., & Jaworski, B. J. (1990). Market orientation: the construct, research propositions, and managerial implications. *The Journal of Marketing, 54*, 1–18.

94.   Koirala, P., (2012). What is Big Data Analytics and its Application in E-Commerce? www.venturecity.com.

95.   Koutsabasis, P., Stavrakis, M., Viorres, N., Darzentas, J. S., Spyrou, T., & Darzentas, J. (2008). A descriptive reference framework for the personalisation of e-business applications. *Electronic Commerce Research, 8*, 173–192.

96.   Krippendorff, K. (2004). Reliability in content analysis. *Human Communication Research, 30*, 411–433.

97.   Kung, D. S., Gordon, L. C., Lin, F., Shayo, C., & Dyck, H. (2013). IT-based System with Dynamic Pricing Algorithm. Business Journal for Entrepreneurs: Business Analytics.

98.   Lane, J., (2012). O Privacy, Where Art Thou?: Protecting Privacy and Confidentiality in an Era of Big Data Access. *Chance, 25*(4), 39–41.

99.   LaValle, S., Lesser, E., Shockley, R., Hopkins, M. S., & Kruschwitz, N. (2011). Big Data, Analytics and the Path from Insights to Value. *MIT Sloan Management Review, 52*, 21–32.

100. Leavitt, N. (2013). Bringing Big Analytics to the Masses. *Computer, 46*, 20–23.

101. Leloup, B., & Deveaux, L. (2001). Dynamic pricing on the internet: theory and simulations. *Electronic Commerce Research, 1*, 265–276.

102. Liebowitz, J. (2013). *Big data and business analytics.* Boca Raton: CRC Press.

103. Lim, E. P., Chen, H., & Chen, G. (2013a). Business Intelligence and Analytics: Research Directions. *ACM Transactions on Management Information Systems, 3*, 17.

104. Lim, M.K., Bahr, W., Leung, S.C., (2013b). RFID in the warehouse: A literature analysis (1995–2010) of its applications, benefits, challenges and future trends. *International Journal of Production Economics, 145*(1).

105. Loebbecke, C., & Picot, A. (2015). Reflections on societal and business model transformation arising from digitization and big data analytics: a research agenda. *The Journal of Strategic Information Systems, 24*, 149–157.

106. Loveman, G. (2003). Diamonds in the data mine. *Harvard Business Review, 81*, 109–113.

107. Manyika, J., Chui, M., Brown, B., Bughin, J., Dobbs, R., Roxburgh, C., Byers, A.H., (2011). Big data: The next frontier for innovation, competition, and productivity. McKinsey Global Institute.

108. Martin, K.E., (2015). Ethical Issues in the Big Data Industry. *MIS Quarterly Executive 14*, 67–85.

109. McAfee, A., Brynjolfsson, E., Davenport, T.H., Patil, D.J. and Barton, D., (2012). Big data. The management revolution. *Harvard Business Review, 90*(10), 61–67.

110. Melville, N., Kraemer, K., & Gurbaxani, V. (2004). Review: information technology and organizational performance: an integrative model of it business value. *MIS Quarterly, 28*, 283–322.

111. Minelli, M., Chambers, M., & Dhiraj, A. (2013). *Business analytics* (pp. 99–125). Big Data, Big Analytics: Emerging Business Intelligence and Analytic Trends for Today's Businesses.

112. Mithas, S., Lee, M. R., Earley, S., Murugesan, S., & Djavanshir, R. (2013). Leveraging big data and business analytics. *IT Professional, 15*, 18–20.

113. Narver, J. C., & Slater, S. F. (1990). The effect of a market orientation on business profitability. *The Journal of Marketing, 54*, 20–35.

114. Nelson, R. R., Todd, P. A., & Wixom, B. H. (2005). Antecedents of information and system quality: an empirical examination within the context of data warehousing. *Journal of Management Information Systems*, *21*, 199–235.

115. Ngai, E. W. T., & Wat, F. K. T. (2002). A literature review and classification of electronic commerce research. *Information Management*, *39*, 415–429.

116. Ngai, E. W. T., Moon, K. K. L., Riggins, F. J., & Yi, C. Y. (2008). RFID research: an academic literature review (1995-2005) and future research directions. *International Journal of Production Economics*, *112*, 510–520.

117. Ngai, E. W. T., Xiu, L., & Chau, D. C. K. (2009). Application of data mining techniques in customer relationship management: a literature review and classification. *Expert Systems with Applications*, *36*, 2592–2602.

118. Nunan, D., & Di Domenico, M. (2013). Market research and the ethics of big data. *International Journal of Market Research*, *55*, 505–520.

119. Ohata, M., & Kumar, A. (2012). Big data: a boon to business intelligence. *Financial Executive*, *28*, 63–64.

120. Orlikowski, W. J. (2007). Sociomaterial practices: exploring technology at work. *Organization Studies*, *28*, 1435–1448.

121. Orlikowski, W. J., & Scott, S. V. (2008). 10 sociomateriality: challenging the separation of technology, work and organization. *The Academy of Management Annals*, *2*, 433–474.

122. Pantelis, K. & Aija, L., (2013, October). Understanding the value of (big) data. In Big Data, 2013 IEEE International Conference on (pp. 38–42). IEEE.

123. Porter, M. E., & Millar, V. E. (1985). How information gives you competitive advantage. In *Harvard Business Review*, *63, 149–160*. Reprint: Service.

124. Rajpurohit, A., (2013). Big data for business managers—Bridging the gap between potential and value, Big Data, 2013 I.E. International Conference on. IEEE, pp. 29–31.

125. Riggins, F. J. (1999). A framework for identifying web-based electronic commerce opportunities. *Journal of Organizational Computing and Electronic Commerce*, *9*, 297–310.

126. Russom, P., (2011, September). The three Vs of big data analytics. TDWI Best Practices Report, Fourth Quarter. 18:1–35.

127. Schneier, B., (2013). The US Government has betrayed the internet. we need to take it back. The Guardian. Sept 5, 2013.

128. Schroeck, M., Shockley, R., Smart, J., Romero-Morales, D., & Tufano, P. P. (2012). *Analytics: The real-world use of big data*. NY, USA: IBM Institute for Business Value.

129. Shah, S., Horne, A., Capellá, J., (2012). Good data won't guarantee good decisions. *Harvard Business Review 90*, 23–25.

130. Shanks, G., Sharma, R., Seddon, P., Reynolds, P., (2010). The impact of strategy and maturity on business analytics and firm performance: A review and research agenda. ACIS 2010 Proceedings.

131. Sharma, R., Mithas, S., & Kankanhalli, A. (2014). Transforming decision-making processes: a research agenda for understanding the impact of business analytics on organisations. *European Journal of Information Systems, 23*, 433–441.

132. Smith, R., & Shao, J. (2007). Privacy and E-commerce: a consumer-centric perspective. *Electronic Commerce Research, 7*, 89–116.

133. Szongott, C., Henne, B. and von Voigt, G., (2012, June). Big data privacy issues in public social media. In Digital Ecosystems Technologies (DEST), 2012 6th IEEE International Conference on (pp. 1–6). IEEE.

134. Spiggle, S. (1994). Analysis and interpretation of qualitative data in consumer research. *Journal of Consumer Research, 21*, 491–503.

135. Strawn, G. O. (2012). Scientific research: how many paradigms? *Educause Review, 47*, 26.

136. Tankard, C. (2012). Big Data Security. *Network Security, 2012*, 5–8.

137. The Economist, (2011). Building with big data: The data revolution is changing the landscape of business. Available at: http://www.economist.com/node/18741392 (Accessed 2nd of March, 2016).

138. Vaidhyanathan, S., & Bulock, C. (2014). Knowledge and dignity in the era of "big data". *The Serials Librarian, 66*, 49–64.

139. Vaithianathan, S. (2010). A review of E-commerce literature on India and research agenda for the future. *Electronic Commerce Research, 10*, 83–97.

140. Viaene, S., & Van den Bunder, A. (2011). The secrets to managing business analytics projects. *MIT Sloan Management Review, 53*, 65–69.

141.   Wagner, E. (2012). Realities learning professionals need to know about analytics. *T+D*, *66*, 54–58.

142.   Waller, M. A., & Fawcett, S. E. (2013). Data science, predictive analytics, and big data: a revolution that will transform supply chain design and management. *Journal of Business Logistics*, *34*, 77–84.

143.   Wamba, S. F., Akter, S., Edwards, A., Chopin, G., & Gnanzou, D. (2015). How 'big data'can make big impact: findings from a systematic review and a longitudinal case study. *International Journal of Production Economics*, *165*, 234–246.

144.   White, M. (2012). Digital workplaces vision and reality. *Business Information Review*, *29*, 205–214.

145.   Williamson, O. E. (1979). Transaction-cost economics: the governance of contractual relations. *Journal of Law and Economics*, *22*, 233–261.

146.   Williamson, O. E. (1981). The economics of organization: the transaction cost approach. *American Journal of Sociology*, *87*, 548–577.

147.   Williamson, O. E. (2000). the new institutional economics: taking stock, looking ahead. *Journal of Economic Literature*, *38*, 595–613.

148.   Wixom, B. H., & Todd, P. A. (2005). A theoretical integration of user satisfaction and technology acceptance. *Information Systems Research*, *16*, 85–102.

149.   Wixom, B. H., Yen, B., & Relich, M. (2013). Maximizing value from business analytics. *MIS Quarterly Executive*, *12*, 111–123.

150.   Zeng, D., & Lusch, R. (2013). Big data analytics: perspective shifting from transactions to ecosystems. *IEEE Intelligent Systems*, *28*, 2–5.

151.   Zhao, D. (2013). Frontiers of big data business analytics: patterns and cases in online marketing. *Big Data and Business Analytics*, p. *43*.

Privacy

1. Chellappa, R.K. & Sin R.G. (2005). Personalization versus privacy: an empirical examination of the online consumer dilemma. *Information Technology and Management*, vol. 6, pp. 181 -202.

2. Mascarenhas, O.A., Kesavan, R. & Bernacchi, M.D. (2003). Co-managing online privacy: a call for joint ownership. *Journal of Consumer Marketing*, vol. 20, pp. 686-702.

3. Mekovec, R.(2010). Online privacy: overview and preliminary research. *Journal of Information and Organizational Sciences*, vol. 34, pp. 195-209.

4. Bubaš, G., Oreh ovački, T. & Konecki, M. (2008). Factors and predictors of online security and privacy behavior. *Journal of Information and Organizational Sciences*, vol. 32, pp. 79-98.

5. Castañeda, J.A. & Montoro, F.J. (2007). The effect of Internet general privacy concern on customer behavior. *Electronic Commerce Research*, vol. 7, pp. 117 .

6. McCole, P., Ramsey, E., & Williams, J. (2010) Trust considerations on attitudes towards online purchasing: The moderating effect of privacy and security concerns. *Journal of Business Research*, vol. 63, pp. 1018–1024.

7. Ashworth, L. & Free, C. (2006). Marketing dataveillance and digital privacy: using theories of justice to understand customer's online privacy concerns. *Journal of Business Ethics*, no. 67, pp. 107 -23.

8. Belanger, F., Hiller, J.S. &Smith, W.J. (2002). Trustworthiness in electronic commerce: the role of privacy, security, and site attributes. *Journal of Strategic Information Systems*, vol. 11, pp. 245-270.

9. Kim, D.J., Ferrin, D.L., & Rao, H.R. (2008). A trust-based consumer decision-making model in electronic commerce: the role of trust, perceived risk, and their antecedents. *Decision Support Systems*, vol. 44, pp. 544–564.

10. Chellappa, R.K. & Sin, R.G. (2005). Personalization versus privacy: an empirical examination of the online consumer dilemma. *Information Technology and Management*, vol. 6, pp. 181 -202.

11. Eisen, O. (2010, July). Online security – a new strategic approach. *Network security*, pp. 14-15

12. Yenisey, M.M., Ozok, A., & Salvendy, A. G. (2005, July)"Perceived security determinants in e-commerce among Turkish university students. *Behaviour & Information Technology*, vol. 24, pp. 259-274

Internet shopping

1. Black, G.S. (2005). Is eBay for everyone? An Assessment of Consumer

2. Demographics, SAM Advanced ManagementJournal, winter, Vol. 70 Issue 1.

3. BMRB International (2004) Hadley House, 79-81 Uxbridge Road, Ealing, London, W5 5SU. Internet Monitor Data.

4. Brucks, M. (1985) The effect of product class knowledge on information search behavior. *Journal of Consumer Research*, Vol. 2, pp.1–16.

5. Cassell J. and Bickmore T. (2000) External manifestations of trustworthiness in the interface. *Communications of the ACM December*: 50-56.

6. Fayu Zheng. (2006). Internet shopping and its impact on consumer behavior. University of Nottingham

7. Cox D. and Rich S. (1964). Perceived risk and consumer decision making – the case of telephone survey. J Mark Res; 1 (November): 32-9.

8. Bigne, E. (2005). The Impact of Internet User Shopping Patterns and Demographics on Consumer Mobile Buying Behavior . *Journal of Electronic Commerce Research.*

9. Jarvenpaa, S. L., & Todd, P. A. (1997). Consumer reactions to electronic shopping on the world wide web. *International Journal of Electronic Commerce*, 1, 59–88.

10. Behavioural model

11. Huang, M. (2000). Information load: its relationship to online exploratory and shopping behavior. *International Journal of Information Management* 20: 337–347

12. Peterson, R. A., Balasubramanian, S., & Bronnenberg, B. J. (1997). Exploring the implications of the Internet for consumer marketing. Journal of the Academy of Marketing Science, 25, 329–346.